Confessions
of a
Helmet-Free
Childhood

True-ish Tales of an Analog Upbringing

Cinnia Curran Finfer

D1617235

Confessions of a Helmet-Free Childhood
Copyright © 2020 by Cinnia Curran Finfer

All rights reserved. This book or any portion thereof
may not be reproduced or used in any manner whatsoever
without the express written permission of the publisher
except for the use of brief quotations in a book review.

The Finfer Group, Inc.
info@helmet-freechildhood.com

Printed in the United States of America

Book Design: Carla Green
Photo, page 21: Claudia L. Espinoza

ISBN hardcover   978-1-7343074-0-5
ISBN paperback   978-1-7343074-1-2
ISBN ebook   978-1-7343074-2-9

To Jack and Valerie Curran, for giving me
a most excellent childhood, some of which you
may be reading about for the first time

To Valerie, Tina and Sheila, the three best traveling
companions for the journey that is childhood

To David Finfer, who went half-sies with me
on two kids with remarkable results

To Scott and Natalie Finfer, who handled childhood
with far more grace than I did—I submit proof
that I wasn't born a mom.

Contents

Prologue

Childhood is not a tidy process.

A bundle of impulses and appetites, most of us didn't know why we did things. We just did them—with mixed results. Bouncing through life as best we could, being a kid could be humiliating one day, exhilarating another . . . with a whole lot of ordinary days thrown in between.

Confessions of a Helmet-Free Childhood is a recollection of my messy ascension to adulthood as well as a testament to experiences I had as a result of being a kid in the 1960s and 1970s. I got to do certain things that did not exist for my parents and no longer exist for my kids—lucky me.

Baseball pitcher Vernon Law once said, "Experience is a tough teacher—you get the test first and the lesson later." For me, this was standard operating procedure.

Because by getting it wrong, we find our way to the right.

Took a Face Plant in the Second-Grade War

It's war! The boys and girls of second grade at Traub Elementary have decided to spend recess outwitting members of the opposite sex and taking prisoners, whenever and however possible, to be released during the next day's recess, when we will pick up where the action left off.

As a relatively new kid, I do not buy into the conflict. I like the girls in my class well enough and have no beef with the boys. Somehow, I negotiate to be a neutral party—a horse, actually. I work it so that as a horse, I can go to

either side with messages from the opposing forces with no threat of capture. This makes perfect sense in second grade.

I find this an excellent arrangement. I trot over to the boys and get their demands. I prance back to the girls, deliver the news, get their reply, and return with the boys' rebuttal. Then it's back again with a revised list of issues—all with full diplomatic immunity.

During one of these crossovers, I am stopped in my tracks by Jimmy, the class heartthrob. He has not heard of my special status and thinks I'm making it up on the fly to evade capture. Frozen in a stand of trees by the side of the schoolyard, I plead my case. Jimmy isn't buying it. He doesn't know me well and does not want to be tricked by a girl.

Meanwhile, in my head, I am exhilarated. Like the other girls in my class, I have a stone-cold crush on Jimmy. Maybe it's his bunny-brown eyes, tan skin, and those bangs! Maybe it's his sense of style. After all, he's the only boy who wore a cardigan sweater on class picture day—teal blue at that. But here I am, face to face with Mr. Second Grade, together . . . alone . . . in the woods. While arguing my case for passage, I'm secretly hoping this takes a long time and that someone will see us together.

Meanwhile, Jimmy still isn't buying it, and in loyalty to his gender, gives chase—either to capture me or drive me back deep into Girl Territory.

I think this is great and take off. Little but swift, I give him a literal run for his money. Glancing back to enjoy the view of The Man of My Dreams chasing me, I trip on some vines and fall forward, landing flat on my face in the damp mud.

I must have been knocked out because, the next thing I remember, I'm in the arms of a large schoolyard monitor, someone's mom in charge of keeping some semblance of law and order during recess. Jimmy is at her elbow, clearing the way through a crowd of kids while explaining what just went down.

My hair, forehead, dress, and knees are covered in mud. Blood trails from my nose, across my face, and down my chin and neck to my collar. My parka is coated with a mixture of mud and blood, and I'm not thinking "Ow," I'm thinking, "Mom is going to be so mad that my parka is such a mess."

As the three of us make our way up to the school on this cold spring day, I hear Jimmy recounting my fall to kids who have gathered to see who is being carried in from recess. Having no recollection of what happened, I'm listening to his account. He is clearly enjoying the attention of being the sole eyewitness to my face plant and assures everyone it was something to behold, reenacting the impact of my face on the ground with a hinged clap of his two hands.

The look of alarm on my homeroom teacher Miss Brockman's face as she enters the nurse's office tells me I took a pretty good fall. Jimmy is there too, being debriefed by the monitor, school nurse, and assistant principal, making some sort of official statement. What I'm also piecing together, because we couldn't be seen from the main yard, is that Jimmy had to run for help. He came to my rescue, alerted the authorities, and led the search team. This thought helps me get through the stinging delivery of Bactine® on my scrapes, as well as the indignity of the insertion of rolled tissues into both nostrils and another piece of tissue under my upper lip to stay the bleeding.

The nurse cleans my legs, hands, and face and calls my mom.

Jimmy steps over to my cot, and I let out a thin, "Thanks, Jimmy." He gives me a dignified nod, like the sheriff in a spaghetti Western, and walks back to class with Miss Brockman, confident that all is well.

Next day, war resumes. Not only do I retain my diplomatic status, but I get major street cred with the girls for even speaking with Jimmy, let alone having him chase me. He may have not known me two days ago, but he does now.

Gamed Pin the Tail on the Donkey

I am not a gambler by nature, but happy to embrace a shortcut.

Birthday parties are a highlight of my social life, and I am an enthusiastic guest. I love being with a crush of school and neighborhood friends as well as getting in on the birthday cake and ice cream. It's a rare kid who gets to invite the entire class to his or her party. Most celebrations involve six to ten kids, depending on how many can fit around the family's kitchen table, along with the birthday kid's brothers and sisters. Balloons, crepe paper streamers, and colorful paper plates and napkins set the mood.

Pin the Tail on the Donkey is a standard game at birthday parties—along with Duck, Duck Goose; Red Light, Green Light; What Time Is It, Mr. Fox?; and at a larger lawn party with lots of kids, Red Rover, Red Rover. Pin the Tail involves a poster-size illustration taped to the family room or basement wall at chest height of a donkey without a tail. Each kid gets a numbered paper tail with either a piece of tape or (for potentially edgier results, including holes in the wall, furniture and/or fellow guests' clothing) a thumbtack. The host blindfolds the guests, one by one, and spins them in one direction, in reverse, and in the original direction again; then they release the child in the general direction of the donkey picture.

Dizzy from spinning, each child staggers and sways (to the great amusement of the other guests) in what he or she thinks is the right direction. Arms extend both to protect yourself from crashing into furniture and locate the wall with the donkey so you can "pin" or tape your numbered tail. As soon as your hand touches the wall, you must plant the tail on where you guess the donkey's rear end is located. Then you can take off the blindfold to see just how off the mark you are—again, a great source of laughs.

The child whose paper tail lands closest to the correct location wins the game. For your effort, you get bragging rights—no trophy, ribbon, or bag of candy and low-grade toys—just the pleasure of telling your parents, as you slide into your Country Squire station wagon at pickup, that *you* won Pin the Tail on the Donkey.

I am second to last in line for this game, which allows me time to watch the other kids play and take in the room and location of the poster. I have no great master plan and quietly space out as I bide my time before my turn. I only realize after I'm blindfolded how much information

I've taken in. Spun and then released, the back of my heel strikes the curved edge of the braided rug, which helps orient me. The sun on the back of my head gives me a sense of how close I am to the wall.

Dizzy, I try to walk as straight as possible. Being a lefty, the paper tail is in my left hand, which is also the side of the poster where the donkey's backside is located. As I make contact with the wood paneling, my right hand lands squarely on the paper of the poster, but my left hand lands on the edge of the poster. I can feel the slight curl of the poster away from the wall. Having stood in line so long, I know exactly how far in the donkey's rear end is from the left edge of the poster, and I quickly plant my tail. Pulling the blindfold off, I am only an inch and a half from a perfect plant—*far* closer than any of my opponents, some of whom hadn't even landed on the paper. I win!

Flush with victory, I enjoy the rest of the games, cake, and ice cream, but I am more excited by the realization that I have cracked a code. With my hand on the edge of the poster, it was so easy to estimate where to put the tail. This is the start of a sensational season of birthday parties, with me getting a bit of a reputation for being a ringer on Pin the Tail on the Donkey. The trick now is to back off on my precision, making my wins appear as organic as possible. Happily, the parties are infrequent enough that no one has the time, energy or interest to watch how I win.

It is best to retire from a crime before being found out.

Lied My Way into Pet Ownership

My favorite place in Bloomfield Hills, Michigan, is a family farm a short walk from our house. It is my oasis. I am cordial with Joe, the boy my age, but solid friends with his younger sister, Lucy. This gives me passage to sledding down their significant hill; chasing chickens and collecting eggs; playing fetch with their dogs; enjoying their well-stocked, oversized sandbox; petting and feeding the two horses; playing in the hayloft; eating wild blackberries in their field; and playing with litters of kittens each spring.

This arrangement is heaven on earth to me and agreeable to my parents. I have access to animals and activities straight out of a Norman Rockwell painting—and it all stays down the street.

I love it all but find singular joy in having a mob of kittens crawl all over me, clawing my skull, biting my fingers, and using me as their personal play structure. The harsh reality is that after two months' time, these kittens all need to find a home. Animal lovers to the bone, the family simply can't continue to absorb an ever-increasing population of cats. Word is put out that a new bunch of free kittens is available, and one by one, my playmates depart for new homes—glad for them, sad for me.

One year, I become particularly attached to a little grey kitten—not particularly great looking but an incredible spirit. He's feisty and curious but also affectionate. When talk of putting out the free kitten alert begins, my heart sinks. I cannot bear the thought of never seeing this cat again. So as is my typical MO, I decide that this kitten is coming home with me.

I lie to my dear friend's mother's face that a conversation with my parents has been had, I have permission to bring a kitten home, and this is the one I want. When the sun starts to set, I scoop my little favorite into my arms and head home. Drunk with the thrill of having my own pet, I think about how great it will be to come home to my own cat, how he'll sleep on my bed . . . and . . .

The sight of my mom talking to a neighbor in our front yard slaps me back into reality. I do *not* have permission to take this kitten. My mom is far from an animal lover and, with four school-age kids, isn't looking for a new responsibility.

I place the kitten in the half-pipe of a neighbor's storm drain for safekeeping and toss my Super Ball® in for its amusement, while I summon my courage to face my mom. As I approach her, true tears well in my eyes as I really want this cat to be ours. I start with a crazy opener . . .

"Mom, you see that kitten?" I ask in a whisper, pointing to the tiny, mewing speck rolling happily in the gravel in the pipe. Her eyes meet mine as I clearly state, "It followed me home."

Only nine weeks old, no kitten would have had the energy or focus to make the trip, but I insist it's the God-honest truth, and, "Can't it please live with us?" My mom needs this like a hole in the head, but her inherent decency isn't going to allow a baby animal to be left unattended by the side of the road. She tells me to bring the kitten inside.

My heart soars.

Then my mother sits me down, looks me in the eye, and asks why I was allowed to bring the cat home. My heart sinks. It's time to come clean. She's far from pleased to learn I'd told my friend's mother that I had her and Dad's permission to bring a cat home as nothing could be further from the truth. Blinking hard while taking that nugget in, she sternly explains that owning a pet is a big responsibility, and this is not going to be *her* responsibility. Feeding, litter box, grooming—it's all on me.

Like any little kid being dangled something I desperately want, I accept all terms with fervent nods of my head, not having the foggiest sense of what I have just agreed to. Then Mom calls my friend's parents to explain the true nature of the events and to learn what else I'll be expected to do for this creature.

As the sun rose the next day, we weren't just a family—we were a family with a cat!

Faked Illness to Evade a Math Test

Math is not my strongest suit. Bouncing among five different grade schools didn't help matters, and having a flip-in eye that results in occasional double vision and requires bifocals can be considered a variable—but let's not discount my lazy streak and ongoing effort to avoid or delay unpleasantness at all costs.

It's the morning of a third-grade math test, and I am utterly unprepared. I knew it was coming and yet spent the previous afternoon biking with friends, and the evening watching TV and playing with our cat. I have not burned a calorie in preparing for said test. This is not going to go well.

Independent of this, our beloved cat, Patsy, has gotten fleas. Disgusted and not an animal lover, my mother has administered a cursory amount of flea powder to the cat, spray to the affected rooms, and calamine lotion to the children, but my sisters' and my arms and legs bear the proof of the ineffectiveness of this effort.

The school week starts with chapel. I half-listen to announcements and lip-sync prayers and hymns. As I scratch my arms, contemplating how to evade the test, I realize that my itchy arms are my path to freedom.

As we file into our classroom, the teacher instructs us to put our books away and have two sharp pencils available for the morning math test. (This lady is hip to the trick of asking to sharpen your pencil in hopes of eyeballing your classmates' tests on the way to and back from the pencil sharpener.) I slide my books into the cubbyhole under my seat and approach the teacher's desk in the manner of an attorney approaching a judge for a critical sidebar discussion.

"Mrs. Strong, I need to go to the nurse's office."

"Why is that?"

"Well, my cat has fleas . . ."

She is puzzled. So I present my freshly scratched arm as physical evidence and tell her of the challenges at home. I finish with "and so my sisters and I all have bites, and well, it's hard to pray and scratch at the same time."

To my complete horror, Mrs. Strong throws her head back, laughing a deep, hearty laugh. When her head returns to its normal position, she's still fighting a giggle and wiping tears from her eyes. She looks at me and breaks out into an even bigger laugh, fighting back tears again.

What on earth? This is not going as planned. But it gets worse.

"Please, tell the class what you just told me."

What? Tell my class about my family's flea infestation and the resulting effect on my life? Never! I am mortified. I confide in her about a personal family matter—and now I am to share it with the class? I shoot her the most incredulous look a third grader can muster and run out of the room, red-faced and teary, down the hall and into the girls' bathroom, where I lock myself in a stall to regroup.

What just happened? This thing has a life of its own! I hear Mrs. Strong enter the bathroom. She spots my shoes, walks over, and stands in front of the stall.

"I'm sorry. I shouldn't have done that. I shouldn't have asked you to tell the class," whispers Mrs. Strong through the stall door. "I've called your mom, and she's going to meet you in the nurse's office with some lotion for your arms. Once that's done, please come back to class."

With that, she leaves the girls' bathroom and returns to class.

What? You called my mom? No! No! *No!* I wanted to go to the nurse's office, get processed with the other "sick" kids, and take my sweet time returning to class to be sure I miss the math test. There's no need to involve my mom! She's going to be annoyed to say the least.

I shuffle to the nurse's office.

Any child knows his or her mother's state of mind by how she walks. No one has to tell me my mom has arrived. The terse steps toward my cot tell me all I need to know. I look up at my mom, who unbuttons my blouse and produces a bottle of calamine lotion from her purse. She puts the lotion on her hands, rubs some on my chest beneath my undershirt, then quickly rubs my forearms and lower legs. Then she stands me up from the cot, looks me in the eye, and says, "Get back to class."

I make a hasty exit from the nurse's office, but as soon as I round the hall corner, I know there's still time to kill. So I retie my shoes, take a long drink from the drinking fountain, consider the content of the fifth-grade bulletin board, read the small print on the fire extinguisher latched to the hallway wall, re-retie my left shoe, check my reflection in the art class display case before looking at which student did what piece, and carefully tuck my shirt into my pinafore. This consumes just enough time so I can watch the red second hand on the hallway clock swing to the top of the hour accompanied by the period bell, releasing a mass of students into the hallway. This grants me free passage to gym class without having to face the math test—until tomorrow.

Crashed My Sister's Bike

My childhood is populated with many poorly designed items (rusty, exposed nuts and bolts on playground equipment come to mind), but my sister's Schwinn Stingray® bicycle is a thing of beauty. A sinewy array of metal, at once sleek and strong with its sloped handlebars, banana seat, and sissy bar, the Stingray is an expression of speed, even while leaning on its kickstand.

Although warned numerous times to watch my speed riding down our street, I'm a fifth grader who needs to know just how fast I can go. We live in the middle of a gently sloping street that curves to the right onto a flat, perpendicular street. I figure I can get some real speed going, take the turn, and then slowly lose speed.

I dispense with the usual procedure of requesting permission to ride Valerie's bike, figuring this won't take long. I take it out of the garage, down the driveway, and turn right (uphill) on our street to assure I'll achieve maximum downhill momentum.

When I turn the bike around at 3:30 p.m. on a Tuesday afternoon, there isn't a single car on Camelback Drive. I tie a loose shoelace and start peddling while standing to get as much speed as possible. Then I plant my butt in the banana seat and continue to churn the pedals, leaning forward into my work. The wind whips my hair straight back as the pavement zips past my feet. I look down the street to the turn and start plotting where to take the bend.

I neglect to notice a small pile of debris in the middle of the road at the bottom of the hill—a combination of sand, dirt, and the residue of eroding pavement.

As I reach the bottom of the hill, I strike the sand.

The front tire of the bike stops dead in its tracks. I do not.

I am airborne. The bike slides sideways out from under me as I sail over the handlebars and make contact with the street a couple of feet later. Impact is brief but painful. My body drags to a stop on the gravelly pavement.

I find myself in the middle of the street with scrapes on my forehead, the right side of my nose and chin, inside both wrists, and the tops of my thighs just below my shorts; my left knee is scratched, and my right knee is bloody. Obviously, I can't see my face, but I can feel every scrape as I assess the rest of me. Pain and fear grip me at the sight of sand and dirt crushed into my skinned and bloodied limbs. I sit in the middle of the street, staring at my wrists and seriously messed-up play clothes and, in considerable pain, start to cry, puzzled that no one is coming to help me.

The bike!

I spin around to see the Stingray® behind me, front wheel up, frame on the street. It's only five steps to get to it, but my body stings with every motion I make. The good news is the front wheel is intact, the handlebars aren't bent, and the sissy bar is in its original position. But when I pick the Stingray up, I see that the chain guard and frame are badly scraped. I groan and cry out, knowing how furious my sister and parents are going to be with me.

I am a pathetic sight, standing in the middle of the street—scraped, bloody, sandy, and dirty—gripping the handlebars and sobbing onto the banana seat. After having a good wail for two to three minutes, I'm struck again that no one has come out to check on me and no car has driven by—a weirdly quiet Tuesday afternoon.

Utterly dejected, I turn the bike up our street and am sickened by the sight of the deep scrapes on the chain guard that cannot be solved with a quick spit and polish by yours truly.

I reach our house, place the bike in its sanctioned spot in the garage, grateful the kickstand still functions, and head inside to meet my fate.

Destroyed My Friend's Doll

Crissy® dolls are a thing in the 1970s. Girls are through with Chatty Cathy,® and we all have a fistful of Barbies,® but Miss Crissy has something they do not—hair that grows! Well, okay, it doesn't exactly grow, but you can adjust the length of her hair. If you push and maintain pressure on a button on her stomach and pull the ponytail in the center of her head (think "I Dream of Jeannie"/Beyoncé topknot), she can have hair that reaches nearly to her feet! A knob located in the middle of her back allows you to dial the hair back into her head to a variety of lengths. It's a hot ticket, much like the American Girl dolls of today. She is just what every little girl wants to be—pretty with beautiful hair.

My friend Carol gets a Crissy doll for her birthday. Not big into dolls myself, I have to say I am impressed. She is large like a baby doll but dressed like a groovy, undersized teenager—and the hair is fantastic! It is understandably Carol's prized possession, and I am one of the few friends she lets play

with it. We concoct some dopey story lines that require changing her clothes, removing her shoes, and of course a new hair length—short for the beach, long for the Big Night Out.

While playing out one of these scenarios, the hair gets stuck in the long setting. We cannot get it to retract shorter than mid-back. We both take a shot at it, working the knob back and forth, holding Crissy® upside down, hoping to release something. While I firmly hold her on the edge of a coffee table, Carol applies her father's adjustable wrench to the knob—nothing. Consulting a grown-up does not enter our thinking.

I propose another approach: Why don't we cut Crissy's hair? Carol is horror-struck. I reason that although this would be bad for a Barbie doll, she's a Crissy doll with apparently an endless supply of hair in her head.

Carol needs to mull it over. Frustrated by the impasse and wanting Crissy to have shorter hair for our next adventure, we agree this is the only way to move forward. And so, using two pair of scissors, we snip off a good three inches of hair—with a haphazard trim line. Happy for a while, we then decide that Crissy now needs longer hair. Carol pushes the button and pulls out three more inches of hair. We concur that it should be longer, so Carol pushes Crissy's torso again—but no more hair. She tries again—no luck.

We agree to a team effort: me on the button, Carol on the hair. She tugs three times and then dissolves into tears, realizing our mistake and that her Crissy can never have floor-length hair ever, ever again. I am sick to see her so upset and crushed with guilt that I am a major player in damaging her favorite toy.

Hearing Carol cry, her mother comes down to check on things and sees the discarded scissors, wrench, and three-inch clumps of doll's hair on the basement floor. She puts things together pretty quickly.

"Why did you cut her hair?" she demands.

"Because Miss Crissy's hair grows!" Carol wails.

She collapses in her mother's arms, sobbing; her mother looks at me incredulously, and I feel worse than a convicted murderer. I am The Friend Who Ruined Everything. The visit ends with a call to my mom that I will be coming home sooner than later. Carol's mom sits us down and explains the limitations of the doll and that what was done cannot be undone. I now start to cry, and Carol watches me, too crushed with loss for any sympathy.

I have steered clear of dolls ever since.

Challenged a Bus Route Bully

Every school bus route has its own social landscape, with its rulers and subjects, tight friends, and loners but, in reality, mostly kids who just want to get from point to point.

But there are those bigger, older, stronger, or weirdly aggressive characters—bored in transport—who feel the need to bide their time by sharpening their claws on someone less confident.

As a perpetual new kid (a fifth grader now at my fourth school), I've had more than my fair share of bus route torment. Being little for my age and far from athletic,

having an unusual name, wearing glasses, and sporting an exotic dental appliance, I am a rich target for some mean-spirited stuff. So I've learned to dodge, to lay low, to avoid—all in the name of a peaceful existence. As a result, I hate bullies. I get that you can't expect everyone to like everyone, but to go out of your way to make someone feel menaced or miserable is beyond the beyond.

My sister has a friend, Liz, a quiet, sweet-tempered kid, a top student who bothers no one. She's coming over to our house after school, and so she and my sister are sitting together on the bus—Val at the window, Liz on the aisle. Then, for no reason at all, Herbie, a neighborhood tough guy, decides to tease Liz about her hair, her face, how she talks, and her pale skin. She stays quiet, enduring his crap, but I notice her face becoming flush. Herbie does too and doubles down, putting his face closer to Liz's and saying even more vile things. I'm burning inside but sit still. But then, sitting behind my sister, diagonal to Liz, I see a single tear track down the side of her flushed cheek—and I lose it.

"Leave her alone!" I hiss.

Herbie looks up, surprised, but not threatened in the least.

I lean in, "Leave . . . her . . . alone," I repeat.

Herbie's face is now nose to nose with me.

"Whadaya gonna do about it?"

My heart is in my shoes. I have nothing, but I stand my ground.

"Ya wanna fight about it?" Herbie snarls.

And for some reason, I say "Yeah!"

Well, we are not going to get into it on the bus as that comes with a host of consequences neither of us wants to navigate. We get off at our stop, and Herbie squares off in front of me.

"I gotta change my clothes," I stammer. "I'll meet you at your house!"

Lucky for me, Herbie agrees to these bizarre terms. I get home and change out of a dress into matching Danskin pants and long-sleeve mock turtleneck.

"You don't have to do this," Valerie says. I sigh and put on fresh socks and my PF Flyers.

As I head down the block, I figure I'm probably in for a couple of hits, which will hurt, but then it will be over. My family gets along okay with Herbie's family. They have a trampoline that they let neighborhood kids use, and although we aren't great friends, we are not enemies. But Herbie had been super mean, making Liz cry for no reason, and well, that's just not right. I said I would fight— game on.

I step up to their front door, pause, and ring the bell. Herbie's older brother Mark, a high schooler, answers. Puzzled to see me at the front door, as it's generally understood that kids can just walk into the backyard to access the trampoline, Mark cocks his head.

"Hi, Cinnia, what's up?"

"I came to fight Herbie."

Mark blanches, blinks, and swallows a smile. "You came to *fight* Herbie?"

I stare straight ahead into the living room and see Herbie lying on his stomach, watching TV.

"He knows what it's about."

Mark is enjoying my stoic delivery. Still holding the doorknob, he yells over his shoulder, "Hey, Herbie, uh, Cinnia is here to fight you."

Herbie looks at the doorway, sees me, rolls his eyes, gets up, and walks to the door. In that instant, I realize he has forgotten about our kerfuffle, and had I not come to

27

his house, this may have all blown over. But what happened happened. I have pronounced my intentions. This is a go.

Herbie steps out of the house, closing the door in his brother's face, brushes by me, and steps down off the stoop into the yard. *Oh, man, here we go*, I think. However, I am mildly pleased that I will be taking a punch on grass rather than on a brick walkway. Uninitiated in fistfights, I wait for Herbie to make the first move. (Admittedly this is a terrible strategy, but I am from an all-girl family and fistfights aren't a thing in our house.) He shifts his weight from foot to foot, clearly weighing his options.

He lunges forward and, putting his face close to mine, snarls, "Get off my lawn, bitch!" He stomps to his front door, flings it open, and then slams it behind him, leaving me in the yard alone, without a scratch.

I stand there, absorbing the moment. It's the first time I've been called a bitch to my face—not a wonderful thing but a big improvement over a fist to the chin or being thrown to the ground. Weighing his options, Herbie probably thought things would get worse for him if he hit a girl but saved face by swearing at me and stomping off. I, on the other hand, have shown up, prepared to do what I said I was going to do. Even better, I have his older brother as a witness who no doubt will delight in retelling this story.

I think we both consider it a win.

Trespassed into a Museum Exhibit

Grade-school romance is an odd animal. Way more energy is spent on the run-up than the actual event. Prior to official boy/girlfriend-hood, there is enormous I-think-he-likes-you/I-think-she-likes-you-back speculation, notes passed, and whispers with friends as well as a major dose of teasing from non-friends. But in daily practice, it means you sit together at lunch, spend time together during recess, and go to each other's homes to play and eat dinner. Being from an all-girl family, there was a singular

joy in walking around the playground shoulder to shoulder with My Guy.

As a sixth grader in Minnesota, I am in the first flush of romance with a boy named Pat. He's a calm kid with a great sense of humor. One afternoon, we ride his school bus home, check in with his mom, and have a snack and then she drops us off at the nearby Museum of History. Maybe it's a free day, maybe she has a friend at the front desk—all I know is there are no tickets involved. We walk in like we own the place.

We are not intellectuals. The museum is just a clean, warm, and safe place for us to spend time, and hey, we might even learn something. We have no plan—we wander past antiquities, run up stairs, hide and startle each other, find our way through the maze of exhibitions, admire weaponry, and giggle at nudity.

We come upon a set of three period vignettes of furniture or, to eleven-year-olds, rooms missing a wall with old-timey furnishings. They are beautifully intricate and authentic, with great care to not only recreate the room but what the view out the window in that era might be. We point things out to each other and marvel at the fanciness of it all. A formal English dining room grabs us. It's so terribly elegant, with ornate goblets and an enormous chandelier—fit for a king and queen.

Pat places his hand on the cord that is meant to keep visitors away from the exhibit, looks at me, and lifts it ever so slightly. I know exactly what he's thinking, but my eyes flare at the audacity of it. He looks both ways down the hall, and there's no one in sight (not surprising at three-ish on a weekday). He holds the cord up a little more and motions with his head to duck under it. I look up and down the hallway again—no one in sight. And so I cat step past the frame of the exhibit.

Pat follows me under the cord, and then we tippy-toe in opposite directions to the head and foot of the table. We are both slender kids and easily slide into the chairs without moving them. We sit squarely with our arms on the chair arms. This is so cool. Pat pantomimes a toast to me and I return it, blowing a kiss and pretending to chat with our imaginary guests while fixing my ornate hairdo. We then both sit back in our enormous chairs, smiling at each other, drunk with success at this crazy move. We touch nothing on the table and are careful with the placement of our feet.

After about three minutes, we both know we'd better get out of there. We slip back to the spot where we entered. Pat holds the cord for me to exit, and I return the favor. Five steps away from the exhibit, we both burst out laughing and quickly move on to another part of the museum.

Today, with security cameras and motion detectors, two kids could never do this.

But we did.

Stole Fireworks

In Ohio, we live next to a family of four boys. The three eldest boys—Rick, Marty, and Jim—are the powerhouse of the high school football team and solid celebrities in our school and town. Why, we need only tell the carpool moms *who* we live next door to, and they all know where to go. Their tail-ender brother, Ray, is my sisters' and my go-to playmate and partner in crime.

Their mother adores my sisters and me—a welcome break from a house full of men. She loves having any configuration of us over to their house and has no problem with us walking in without ringing the doorbell or knocking.

She gives us all access to their home and yard. We chat in the kitchen, help around the house, or play Monkey in the Middle while the older boys play catch in the driveway.

My dad has advised us that playing with high school boys comes with risks. If we aren't willing to operate at their level, it's best not to play at all. We, of course, completely ignore this as it is way too fun to be able to hang out with them.

My sisters and I are not angels, especially when it comes to our oversized neighbors. When the three older boys collapse in their den from an exhausting football practice, we are active nuisances while they try to recover. We think it great fun to grab sections of their hair and twist-tie rubber bands around them, creating a haystack effect across their heads. We also grind Cheetos® into their teeth or tie their shoelaces together as they attempt to snooze on the couch or the floor. Much like sleepy lions tolerate small birds picking bugs from their skin and eyes, they endure our semi-torture until one playfully lunges at us and we run, fake screaming, out of the room, only to return and press our luck again.

For reasons I cannot explain to this day, I decide to take it to a new level. Gainfully employed at the local Dairy Queen,® Jim has amassed a fairly impressive fireworks collection (Roman candles, M-80s, and similar armaments) and has unwisely shown it all to me, bragging about its financial value.

I think it would be hilarious to take all of it just to see the look on his face.

Bad idea.

Jim's nickname for me is Titmouse (FYI, a small songbird native to North America but applied to me because I'm both small and undeveloped). Whereas another girl might take offense, I take it in stride. It's usually delivered with nonchalance: Jim greets me with "Hey, Titmouse!" as I walk up my driveway from the bus stop. Or while playing in a friend's yard, he yells out of a car: "Titmouse, your mom is looking for you." I guess I kind of like it. Jim is a big-deal football player, and I am a middle school nobody.

So one afternoon, I take *all* of his fireworks (three trips) from his bedroom closet to our basement crawl space. I'm careful with the various-shaped boxes and store them in a corner I know is dry and where no harm will come to them (as I plan to return everything).

You can imagine Jim's dismay at finding his secret cache gone. When he puts it together that I am the only one who has access to the house and knows where everything is stored, he storms downstairs where his brother Ray and I are playing Battleship and snarls, "Where are they, Titmouse! Give them back now!"

Stupidly, I decide to stonewall but secretly enjoy seeing him so unnerved.

"I don't know what you are talking about," I reply.

He marches Ray and me up to his room and points to the empty closet. His older brothers hear the commotion and enter the bedroom to watch the proceedings, mildly stunned that I am named in the crime.

"They were here this morning. What did you do with them?" he presses. "Tell me where they are now, or we (pointing to his older brothers) are going to give you a pink belly until you tell."

Marty and Rick look as surprised as I do at this announcement.

(Pink belly: a popular schoolyard punishment where a kid is held to the ground while his or her stomach is repeatedly slapped to the point where the skin is somewhat chapped and tender to the touch. It's unpleasant and takes a day or two to fully recover.)

I'm not talking, assuming he is bluffing.

He is not bluffing.

As I try to charge out the door, Rick and Marty take me by the arms and legs (I weigh about 70 pounds, so this is snap for them to do) and hold me in place on the bed, while Jim lifts the front of my shirt to expose my stomach and administers a pink belly. They are careful with me. It's a half-hearted delivery, more for show than enforcement, but Jim wants to make a point. After about 10 slaps, he stops and nods to his brothers to release me, giving me an opportunity to come clean.

Nothing doing—I make a run for the bedroom door. One of the brothers reaches to stop me but catches the sleeve of the white, button-down shirt I'm wearing and, in doing so, tears it at the arm seam, which rips almost completely off the body of the shirt. I run down the hallway to the open staircase, holding my stomach because it does sting, my shoulder exposed due to the ripped sleeve, and take the stairs as fast as I can with all three high school boys running after me . . . just as their mother enters the house with two bags of groceries in her arms. Barely into her home, she looks up to see a sixth-grade girl racing down the stairs from a bedroom, holding her stomach with a ripped shirt and her three teenage boys in hot pursuit.

"*What is going on?!*" she yells.

Everyone freezes in their tracks.

"They gave me a pink belly!" I scream.

"*What . . . is . . . a . . . pink . . . belly?*" bellows their mom.

I dramatically lift my shirt to reveal the redness from being repeatedly slapped, confess to taking Jim's fireworks, and say that he's done this with his brothers' help to get me to tell where my hideout is. She is so relieved to learn this is just a prank gone sideways, rather than what the disturbing optics suggest, that she lets out a little laugh and ushers us into the den to sort things out.

I did return the fireworks, but it's a damaging event to my previously breezy relationship with Jim. I am no longer just the somewhat annoying little girl next door. I am now a capable thief with knowledge of his home.

Weaponized Water Balloons

We are usually a home-for-the-holidays kind of family, but one December, my dad goes big and springs for a family vacation in Florida. Grateful for a break from the Midwestern snow, my sisters and I find ourselves in a double-queen bedroom in a tall hotel, with white sand and palm trees below.

Although we all love the warm weather, the pool, and the ocean, my older sister and I quickly suss out that there's not a lot for a seventh and eighth grader to do. Too old for the children's programming, and way too young to order a drink, my mom encourages Valerie and me to check out

the "teen center." This is a sorry state of affairs consist-
ing of a windowless, cinderblock room painted yellow with
some secondhand hotel furniture and a tired-looking juke-
box. Stevie Wonder's "Superstition" blares as we review
the selection of 45s (small vinyl records containing a hit on
one side and usually a marginal song on the "B" side). Our
fellow teens look as miserable as we are to be sentenced to
this space. The dreariness of the room drives us away.

So we convene with nature, swimming in the ocean and
sunbathing, but I don't think any of us enjoy the crush of
humanity when dining or the crowded rides up and down
the elevator. A Christmas vacation is a rare treat, and we
should enjoy it. But face it: We are bored.

One morning, crossing the hotel lobby with my two
younger sisters, I spy an open ballroom door revealing a
crew installing New Year's Eve decorations. Ladders and
boxes of supplies containing streamers, noisemakers, card-
board hats, tiaras, and tons of balloons line the walls. While
admiring the installers' work, the three of us grab enough
balloons to fully stuff our shorts pockets.

We walk with our hands still in our pockets to the elevator and return to our room, emptying the balloons onto
the bed. We amuse ourselves for a while keeping one balloon aloft among the three of us for as long as we can,
but that quickly loses its charm. So we start making water
balloons to throw at each other on the hotel room balcony.
We close the sliding glass door to keep the water out of the
room.

We screech and scream as we evade one impact, only to
get soaked a second later as a balloon explodes on contact,
soaking our clothes as it releases the water with a splat.
Then one balloon misses its mark and goes sailing eleven

stories down to the service area below, leaving an impressive splash mark along with its tattered remains.

Now here's a fun idea! My sisters and I race to the bathroom to fill more balloons and gleefully laugh as our water bombs crash below with varying effects. Two accidently splash a delivery driver just as he gets out of his truck, splattering his trousers with grime from the driveway. This is not skill; it's by chance. He looks up, sees us, and gives us a middle finger.

We retreat to the room, bent over in laughter. Figuring we shouldn't push our luck too much longer, we agree to do a grand finale: Fill up the remaining balloons, and launch them all at once.

On the count of three, we toss twelve balloons over the railing then peer below to witness the impact. Unfortunately, a hotel employee had exited the loading dock at precisely the wrong moment, with three of the twelve balloons landing on him. Standing still from the shock of the first three balloons places him squarely in the impact zone of the remaining nine. He is soaked to the skin. We gasp and look at each other wild-eyed. I see him look up with his hand moving and realize he's counting floors. I grab my little sisters' hands and tug them out of sight.

Realizing he may come up to reprimand us, we need to be out of the room when he arrives. I order my sisters to change clothes and grab their sunglasses. This is a ridiculous overreaction, but having viewed countless *I Spy*, *Mission Impossible*, and *Get Smart* episodes when a clever change of identity is critical to a clean getaway, I decide that we can't be too careful under these circumstances. I am convinced senior management will be on the way shortly, and we must be unrecognizable.

We hustle out of the room with beach towels and sand toys, take the first elevator down to the lobby, head straight to the beach, and start building a sandcastle/alibi immediately. After about twenty minutes, we figure the danger has passed.

The event went unreported.

Recycled a School Project

Although many kids are guilty of reworking an existing project, rather than starting from scratch, I have the distinct advantage of attending so many schools with so many different teachers and curriculums that if I recycle a project, there's no way to trace it. This particular opportunity keeps presenting itself, and so I keep taking it.

My first round with Thomas Alva Edison takes place at a Catholic elementary school outside Detroit. We are assigned a project on Great Americans. The teacher places a poster on the wall by the door, and we are to sign up for our preferred Great American. The fact that Edison was the inventor of the lightbulb duly impresses my third-grade self, and so I write my name next to this renowned innovator's.

After lunch, I learn that I'm unchallenged in my interest in Edison and can proceed.

My research is based on one book. My deliverables are some handwritten note cards about The Talented Mr. E's "Childhood and Education," "Early Professional Efforts," and "Major Contributions." I enhance this with a poster that displays marginal artistic ability and wear one of my mother's old, black sports jackets as a Thomas Alva Edison "costume" for the five-minute oral presentation, based on highlights from my written report. I present in the first person, recounting Notorious T.A.E.'s success as if I were the Wizard of Menlo Park himself. It all goes well enough. It's not fireworks, but I present the required information in a reasonably engaging fashion.

The following year, I find myself in a progressive public elementary school outside Minneapolis, where my history teacher has assigned us a biography. After the initial groan of having one more thing to do, a lightbulb goes off in my head. Wait a minute!

I have the bones of a biography already done.

I hurry to turn in my request to recount the success of Thomas Alva Edison—and I get it! With two weeks to get it done, I naturally wait till the Wednesday before the Friday it's due, go digging for my old report, then visit our tiny, local library. Being such a high-profile person, there are easily a dozen biographies on my old pal, Mr. E. I beef up the content of my prior report, expand the bibliography, and include photos of him as a lad, young inventor, and the staid, scowling, rumpled, potbellied guy in a vested suit we have all come to identify as The Inventor of the Lightbulb. I go to the drug store to purchase a three-hole project folder and design a cover page—done!

My project does not take the world by storm. It is not even featured on the class bulletin board, mind you. I get a solid B and move on.

The last quarter of sixth grade finds me in a middle school in Cleveland, Ohio. It's rough enough going from a big dog in elementary school to a baby in middle school. To make things worse, my homeroom is populated with some world-class troublemakers. It's all I can do to navigate between the cafeteria and recess without drama, so when I receive a handout assigning us the biography of an American scientist, I immediately request Thomas Alva Edison. At least one thing in my life is going to be easy!

To my delight, I get my old favorite, and the assignment covers well-traveled territory. So I dust off the previous report and add a table of inventions with their dates of introduction and impact on the world. That done, I redesign the cover, freshen up the biography with two recent books, and hand it in.

Again, hardly the report of the year, but I like to think that Thomas Alva would have saluted my inventiveness.

Set the Fondue Kit on Fire

Fondue for dinner is a win-win in our house. It's super easy prep for my mom and the fun of fondue-ing for us—open flame, cubed meat, and bubbling oil—good times! My parents own an attractive ceramic fondue kit ("suitable for entertaining"). Even better, it comes complete with a set of matching fondue forks with assorted tips so you can keep track of who is fondue-ing what.

Mom fills the pot with cooking oil, heats it up on the stove, and then transfers it to the kitchen table on a frame that houses a Sterno® can as a heat source. (When we didn't have Sterno, there was a household agent we used instead. I believe it was either a lacquer or shellac thinner that burned much like Sterno. The fact that I'm still not clear on this is the source of the problem.)

To set up for an evening of fondue-ing, Sheila sets the table, Valerie gets plates out, Tina pours water for the four of us, and Mom asks me to put the fuel in the Sterno holder. Attention to detail not being my hallmark, I open the laundry room

cabinet and grab a canister whose shape and colors I recognize but don't bother reading the label. I figure if it's there, it's the right stuff.

We light the fuel, place the pot over the Sterno, stab our first selection, and place it in the fondue pot. The phone rings, and my mom picks up the kitchen extension.

"Betty! Hi . . . Oh, the girls are just sitting down to fondue. Hold on."

Mom glances over at the table to see that the fondue is up and running, frees the six-foot-plus curly phone cord from around the kitchen island, and steps into the dining room to take the call.

Left on our own, the four of us jockey for best position, warn each other not to eat directly off the fondue fork, and pass the steak sauce . . . until we notice that the flames are getting thicker and spreading across the bottom of the pot, blackening it at a rapid pace.

We all get quiet. This is not normal.

"Uh, Mom? The flames on the fondue pot are kind of big."

"Just adjust the damper so the holes are smaller so less air gets in," Mom instructs us from the dining room.

We do that, but not only does it not lessen the flames— they are growing larger, and the pot is blackening even faster.

"Uh, Mom, that's not working . . . um, Mom, the flames are getting bigger . . . and the pot . . . Mom!"

Mom rounds the corner with the phone still at her ear, clearly annoyed that we are challenged by this simple task.

Then she sees the flames.

Part ninja, part ballerina, she drops the phone, grabs the flour and sugar canisters from the counter, twists back to the table, takes a commanding step forward, and dumps the contents of both onto the flaming fondue kit, extinguishing the flames on contact and sending a mushroom cloud of flour throughout the kitchen.

The relief of the averted disaster is short-lived. Although we are all impressed with her quick thinking and action, that was then, and this is now.

"Who put the fuel in the Sterno can?" she seethes.

"Me."

"Show me what you used."

As soon as I retrieve the can, I realize my terrible mistake. There were two similarly shaped cans in the cabinet with the same graphics (because they're sold by the same company), but one contained shellac thinner and the other was lacquer thinner. I picked the wrong one. After an epic eye roll, I then receive The Withering Look from my mom—you know, the one that delivers five tons of a custom blend of anger and disappointment. She tersely explains what could have happened and the importance of reading labeling before using anything—especially something you are going to set on fire. She's rightly furious, and I have to help clean up.

Have you ever cleaned up flour and sugar off of multiple surfaces? It would have been easier to add some eggs and bake the table.

Took the Fifth in a Food Fight

Food fights are a clear and present danger in middle school. The cafeteria is a loud and messy place on a good day; on bad days, it's a minefield.

Most kids want to get through the cafeteria line without incident, secure a chair at a table with current friends, eat a meal without drama, and have some fun—or at least get some fresh air in the schoolyard—before an afternoon of classes.

Food fights erupt with little or no warning. They can be ignited by someone being pushed in the lunch line, swatting another kid's tray to the floor, or a misguided

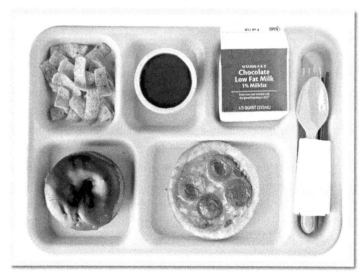

toss of a milk carton meant for the trash can that instead accidentally strikes and spills on someone's shoulder. And sometimes, it's just a sudden, unprovoked melee.

I don't see who started it, but I see what started it.

Some ketchup-sopped French fries sail from behind me, over my table, and land with a splat on the adjacent table populated by eighth-grade boys—but not before depositing some juicy droplets across our table. My friends and I glance at the runny, red drops and look at each other, knowing this is not good. Fire is returned in the form of a deconstructed tuna fish sandwich, which is responded to with a drippy ice cream cup.

Things escalate quickly, with milk cartons, lettuce, and Fritos® all becoming airborne. Caught in the crossfire, my girlfriends' glee or horror at the unfolding events is directly related to how much the flying food is landing on them. I survey the action in between ducking. I see Bob, a big guy from my class, across the room with an apple in his hand. His eyes dart in several directions with his arm in full wind-up; a few more pivots, and then he releases . . .

It's a deer-in-headlights moment for me. I see this flying red dot, getting bigger faster in my direction, and yet I don't move. The apple strikes my left eye. The combination of force and surprise throws me out of my chair and onto the floor, with a sympathetic chorus of "Ohhhhhhhhh!" from the surrounding kids as I descend. The food fight ceases as I hear the scuffle of adult feet in my direction and the screech of lunch chairs being pushed out of the way as they come to my aid. My girlfriends help me to a chair and dust remnants of lettuce, bread, potato chips, and napkins off me as I am grilled for information. Too stunned to talk, I blink hard and hold the left side of my head in my hand.

The authorities want names, and although I am clear about who threw the apple, I say I have no idea because I don't want further retribution. But more to the point, I am absolutely sure that Bob wasn't aiming for me. Our eyes never met as he threw the apple, so I felt it wasn't on purpose (as opposed to some highly targeted tuna fish and pudding), and I don't want the majority of heat to fall on this one kid. The next day I have a major shiner—you know, the deep-purple-to-green bruising around the eye one might sport after a fistfight. My teacher is horrified, and my girlfriends are concerned—yet fascinated—with the changing colors of the bruise. I am the talk of the town.

Later that day, between class periods, I pass Bob, the apple chucker, in the hallway. Our eyes meet only for an instant. We share a sideways glance as we pass each other. His expression tells me he is stunned at the damage done. I also think he seems to feel badly about it. A fringe benefit of this encounter is that I never have any trouble from him for the balance of my time in that school system. He and his friends are big, tough guys who could make your life a misery, but it's never an issue for me.

I guess I paid at the office.

Epilogue

I am grateful for a childhood of remarkable autonomy and, more often than not, a lot of fun. Both buddies and bullies populated my life, and I took my share of hits. But in finding my way through childhood, I learned some major lessons:

- » A dishonest win is never as fulfilling as an honest victory.
- » If you can't figure something out, ask for help.
- » If you are doing something for love, say so.
- » Taking without asking is stealing and will be dealt with accordingly.
- » Delaying dealing with something only lengthens your agony.
- » Even if something happens by accident, it's still on your watch.
- » Being bigger and/or older doesn't assure being smarter.
- » Read the label before igniting anything.
- » When you stand up for someone, the other guy just might stand down.
- » Speed + (dirt + sand + gravel) = scabs.

Acknowledgments

As with everything else important to me, my sisters Valerie Bock, Tina Curran and Sheila Lane were the first three people on the planet to hear about and receive a rough draft of *Confessions*.

A medal of valor should be issued to my husband David Finfer, for enduring the singular insanity that is living with someone who is writing a book.

As payback for decades of encouragingly nagging me to write a book, I trembled as I hit the send button to Joyce Clegg, Kyrian Corona, Monica O'Toole and Peggy Verrege. Of course, I was showered with advice. I considered all of it, incorporated a lot of it and am grateful for the time they gave me.

Once I had a working draft, I had no question who to call to make this idea a reality. Carla Green and I had worked together at the Pacific Design Center in Los Angeles. She was always the low-key, creative and sensible force you want on any project. How fortunate to work with someone who knows the rules of the game but also has a sense of you as a person. She has turned straw into gold at every turn. If that was not enough, Carla introduced me to my editor, Jean-Noel Bassior.

As soon as Jean-Noel saw the chapter titles, she understood what I was up to. It was remarkable to receive the technical and stylistic direction I needed from someone who so thoroughly embraced the spirit of the book. I feared the editing process would be like root canal, but it was more like a friendly game of tennis.

Pam Schroeder, proofreader extraordinaire, helped me face my addiction to crutch words and the overuse of dashes. I hope I have not impaired her vision permanently.

About the Author

After successfully departing from her parents' home, Cinnia Curran Finfer went on to graduate from Endicott College in Massachusetts and American University in Washington, D.C. She has spent her adult life in Southern California. When not contemplating her childhood, she's a marketing communications consultant, wife, and the mother of two grown children. Cinnia currently resides with her husband, David Finfer, in Rancho Mirage, California.

CPSIA information can be obtained
at www.ICGtesting.com
Printed in the USA
FSHW011202260120
66287FS